Love
the joy that wounds

Rumi

Love
the joy that wounds

CALLIGRAPHY BY
Lassaâd Metoui

SOUVENIR PRESS

First published in France by Editions J.C. Lattés as *Amour, Ta Blessure Dans Mes Veines*.
© 2004 Editions Lattés

English edition published 2005
By Souvenir Press Ltd
43 Great Russell Street,
London WC1B 3PD

The extracts in this collection were translated into French from Persian by Mahin and Nahal Tajadad and Jean-Louis Carrière, and into English from the French by Elfreda Powell

Preface © Jean Claude Carriere

The right of Lassaâd Metoui to be identified as the illustrator of this work has been asserted by him in accordance with the Copyright, Designs and Patents Act, 1988

ISBN 0285637320

Typeset by FiSH Books, London
Printed in Singapore by MRM Books

To all the people

who love

and do not know how to express it

Everything – strength, joy and knowledge – comes to us through love. Love burns and devours, love destroys life and it gives life.

Love is both secretive and revelatory.

This is how it was for Jelalaldin Rumi, the thirteenth-century Persian poet, grand master of the Sufi tradition and founder of the brotherhood of Whirling Dervishes.

Born in what is now Afghanistan, then settling in Konya, in Turkey, shielded from the invading Mongol hordes, he was a venerated teacher, an unrivalled scholar. People from everywhere came to listen to him.

Then one day he met a wandering dervish, a man who was very sensitive to the cold, and older than Rumi was. He spoke in riddles, was insolent and irritable, and his name was Shams al-Din of Tabriz. Love blossomed between the two men. They stayed together, locked away, for forty days and forty nights.

When they went their separate ways, Rumi was no longer the academic whom everyone had known. He danced, laughed, made up poems. He had been illuminated, as though from within.

In a lightning flash he had become a poet.

And for the rest of his days, he forgot his professorial chair and his teaching, and, instead, sang of this metamorphosis to the whole world, with unforgettable élan.

In all he wrote some 50,000 lines of poetry, much of it collected together in The Book of Shams al-Din of Tabriz and in the Masnari, two jewels in the world's history of poetry.

Love is a grace, Rumi tells us over and over. It is a fire, it is intoxication, an unceasing turning, a breath from heaven. It is a way for all lost people and a cure for every fever.

And love is limitless, for it excludes nothing and no one. Here, lovers are not alone in the world.

Quite the opposite. To love someone is to love the whole world.

Jean-Claude Carrière

Join us in
our circle

Come and join us in our circle,
We the lovers, we who admire,
So that we can lure you into
The lovely garden of desire.

You are water, whirling water,
Yet still water trapped within,
Come, submerge yourself within us,
We who are the flowing stream.

Come, we are all so lost and strayed,
And in the direst poverty,
And we know of nothing to sing
Except the song of unknowing.

Oh, come into our hostelry

And close up the door from within.

Where do you come from? And from where

Do man's joy and sorrow begin?

Oh, cloud of gentle rain, pour down!

Come, let us friends get truly drunk!

And you, the king of tricksters, come!

Befuddled with drink we all greet you.

Oh you, unceasing sun, to me
Your particles communicate
The luminous essence of God,
Are you our God? I do not know.

Intoxicated, I say nought,
Bewitched by the magic potion.
I cannot differentiate
Between my drunk and sober state.

Oh master come, oh master come!
Oh master, come again, again!
Do not argue, do not argue,
Oh moon, oh wandering moon, come!

You are vision, you are hearing,
Of the whole world, the Chosen One.
You are Joseph who was kidnapped
At the gate of the bazaar. Come!

You are the brightness of the day,
The joy that burns away sadness,
The moon that shines upon the night,
The cloud that bears such sweetness. Come!

Oh you, straying heart, just come!

Oh you, aching liver, just come!

If the path to the gate is closed,

Take the way by the wall, but come!

قمر
العجف الخلف

You are our moon upon this earth,

Our dawn that breaks by night,

Our shield in dangerous times,

My cloud of honeyed rain.

Oh sky, without me, do not change,

Oh moon, without me, do not shine;

Oh earth, without me, do not grow,

Oh time, without me, do not go.

Others give you the name of Love,

And me the sultan of that love.

Higher than such illusions,

Oh, you cannot go, without me.

You are the drop
and the ocean

You are the drop, and the ocean.
    You are kindness, you are anger,
        You are sweetness, you are poison.
            Do not make me more disheartened.

        You are the chamber of the Sun,
        You are the abode of Venus,
        You are the garden of all hope.
        Oh, Beloved, let me enter.

        You are daylight, you are fasting,
        You are the fruit of misery,
        You are water, you are the bowl,
        Oh, give me some water this time.

      You are the grain of wheat, the snare,
     You are the wine, you are the cup,
Raw you are, and cooked too you are.
Oh, do not leave me quite so raw.

You, the sudden resurrection,
You, the everlasting mercy,
You, who comes forth bringing fire
Into the dry wood of my thoughts.

You, the chamberlain of the sun,
You, who merit every hope,
You, whom we seek, and you who seek,
You, the end and the beginning.

Kingdom and sultan you become,
Eden and durwan you become,
Both faith and sin, so you become,
Gazelle and lion you become.

Breath and pulse as one you become,
Seen and unseen, so you become,
Bitter and sweetness you become,
The substance of wine you become.

The skylight of every house,
Of every garden, roses,
Without me, you become Myself,
While you, without you, you become.

Bitter your acts, bitter am I,
  Kindness your deeds, kindness am I,
  Pleasant and gentle, so you are,
    Fine honeyed lips and sweet talker.

You are prime matter, who am I?
The looking-glass in your fingers.
I become all that you display -
The mirror to prove you exist.

Oh master, say what bird I am!
Not a partridge, nor a falcon,
Nor am I good, nor am I foul,
Nor am I this, nor am I that.

Nor the nightingale in the garden,
Nor the great lord of the souk.
Oh master, do give me a name,
A name by which to call myself.

Neither metal nor wax am I,
　Neither slave nor free man am I.
　To none have I given my heart,
　Nor have I taken another's.

　　Come what may, I no longer hold sway,
　　For to a stranger I belong.
　　And wherever he may entice me
　　Invariably I shall go.

You have branded my heart,
It will not err elsewhere.
Without others, I can cope;
Without you, I cannot.

You are my wine, my joy,
My garden, my springtime,
My slumber, my repose,
Without you, I can't cope.

You try to be faithful
And sometimes you're cruel.
You are mine. Then, you leave.
Without you, I can't cope.

And when you take the lead,
I become your footstep.
Your absence leaves a void.
Without you, I can't cope.

You have disturbed my sleep,
You have wrecked my image.
You have set me apart.
Without you, I can't cope.

Love asks us to
enjoy our life

Love asks us to enjoy our life
  For nothing good can come of death.
  Who is alive? I ask.
  Those who are born of love.

  Seek us in love itself,
  Seek love in us ourselves.
  Sometimes I venerate love,
  Sometimes it venerates me.

Love asks us to enjoy our life

I was dead, now I am alive,
    I was a tear, now I can laugh.
        For the joy of love came to me,
            Happy am I for ever more.

                He says: 'You are a candle flame,
                    The focus of the assembly's prayer.'
                    No assembly am I, nor flame,
                    But drifting smoke is what I am.

                He says: 'You have feathers and wings,
                    I give you no wings nor feathers'.
                    I yearn for his feathers, his wings.
                    Wingless and featherless am I.

            You are the source of the sun.
            And I am the willow's shadow.
            Oh, you have struck me on the head,
        Wretch that I am, on fire am I.

All details of the world
  Are lovers. And every
    Detail of the face's
      Universe sings with life.

      But in no way will they
      Let you know their secret:
      Only he who merits
      The forbidden secret.

    Were that the sky were not
    Rapturously in love,
  In no way would there be
Purity in its heart.

Were that the sun itself
Were not full of love's fire.
No shining light would be
Glowing on its beauty.

Were the earth and mountain
Not full of love's sweet glow,
At the heart of neither
Would any green plant grow.

And what if the sea had
Never known love's desire?
In the end it would have
A place to rest somewhere.

When could the lesson that love has

Given at last be forgotten?

Of discourse, gossip and dispute,

Oh yes, we have been delivered.

Should your friend dismiss you,
Do not be disheartened:
Today he rejects you,
Tomorrow he'll relent.

If he has shut you out,
Don't go away. Just stay.
Patience is rewarded.
He will reinstate you.

If he appears to bar
All passageways and paths,
He will open the secret way
For you, which others do not know.

———

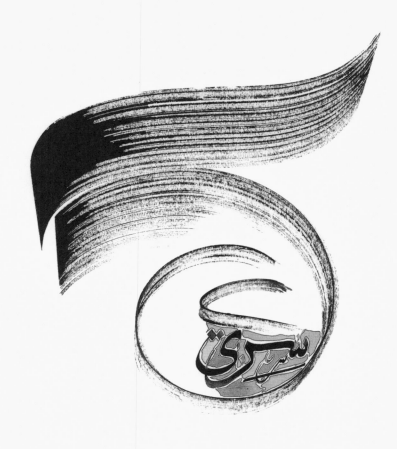

To the wind shall
I scatter you

To the wind shall I scatter you

You have fallen in love with me.
　　To the wind shall I scatter you.
　　　Listen to me.
　　　　I warn you now, build up no hopes,
　　　　　Believe me, I shall destroy you.
　　　　　Listen to me.

　　　　　If, like the bee and the ant, you now
　　　　　Were to build two hundred houses,
　　　　　Oh, I shall still make you homeless,
　　　　　Oh, I shall still make you lonely.
　　　　　Listen to me.

　　　　　For me, you are like a dead bird
　　　　　Held in my hand, at hunting time.
　　　　　And I, the hunter, will make you
　　　　　A lure for all the other birds.
　　　　　Listen to me.

　　　You are guardian of a treasure,
　　Oh, just like a sleeping serpent,
And you shall see, I shall make you
Spin around like that sleepy snake.
Listen to me.

I'll tear apart the seven skies,

And I shall cross the seven seas,

When you, you charmer, look at me:

This distraught soul, My living breath.

For without you, I swear, the town

Has become like a prison to me.

Distraction and the mountain

And the desert, all I desire.

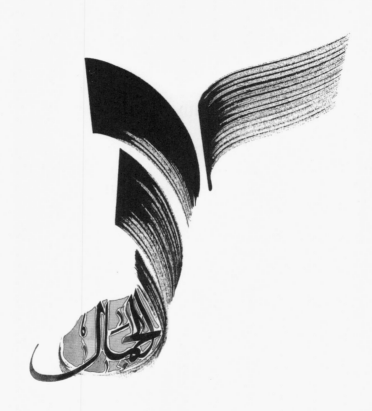

Your heady presence gone,

What use is wine to me?

Without you at my side,

What use it is to roam?

Oh, do not strike the man
Who is my very life,
Who is my very own.
Oh, do not strike him down.

He is my water
And he is my bread.
His garden of hope
Is beyond compare.

And patience flees my heart
And reason flees my mind

And patience flees my heart,

And reason flees my mind.

Oh, how drunk can I get to be,

Without your love's security?

Reason says: 'It is his fault that
I am a dervish, and so sick'.
Love says: 'It is his fault that
I am a mage and trickster.'

Ignorance: 'With no news I am
Like a man cut off from himself.'
Knowledge says: 'As for me, I am,
By far, oldest in the bazaar.'

And Asceticism says: 'I am
Well versed in every secret.'
What has Poverty to impart?
'I have no turban and no heart',

And patience flees my heart

You prey on my reason,

   Your tactic is to fire,

     Set your sights on my life,

     Snare my heart in your net.

   Now, if reason's custodian

   Puts an obstacle in your path,

   Play tricks on him and jink away,

For sure it is not wise to stay.

All living creatures have I fled,
 Of every thing am I now free,
  Invisible and visible.
   So,now, what's the whole world to me?

  Besotted with our union,
  I have no mind for anyone else.
  I am your prey, I am your game.
  What use, now, is my bowmanship?

Desire for your face

    Would split the hardest stone.

    Life takes wing and soars,

    In my joy of having you.

    Fire becomes like water,

    My reason is destroyed.

And imagining you

Kills any hope of sleep.

And patience flees my heart

Oh, enemy of my reason,
    My remedy, my amnesia,
        I am the wine. You drink me in
            As though I could assuage your thirst.

          You are the first, you are the last,
          You are outside, inside my head,
          You are the king, and the sultan,
          And the chamberlain, and the guide.

          You are far away, you are near,
          You are before me, and behind,
          You are the malevolent friend,
          You are the sting and the nectar.

The robber of the selfless-me's,
The meeting-place for dervishes,
Oh, look how ecstatic they are
When you embrace them in your arms.

And patience flees my heart

You, focus of every word,
Oh you, both friend and enemy,
You, who are both eternal life
And, yes, sudden catastrophe.

You plunge into my beating heart,
And yet my heart excuses you,
I care not now if you wound me,
I no longer look for mercy.

Oh, you are a seasoned archer,
So aim your good arrow at me,
For I am your arrow's victim,
For I am your bow's willing slave.

Yes, it is your wound, in my veins
That is life, and yes, that gives life.
And your sword in my living blood
Is, troublingly, king of the world.

When love ripped my pocket awry,

I said: 'Hey, what are you doing?'

Love said: 'Isn't my unending

Bounty enough to satisfy?'

'Oh, where is this heart going,'I cried,
'My so intoxicated heart?'
And then the king of kings replied:
'Be still, it is coming towards you.'

My heart has begun a revolt.
Oh, it has spilt the blood of kings.
My heart is filled with everything,
And yet still it must walk alone.

Hasten, time flies, and it is late,
My heart is sated with the earth,
Liberate it, intoxicate,
To stop it saying: 'Hasten now'.

Give me neither bread nor water,
Give me no rest, nor any sleep.
For the thirst to possess your love,
Is worth my blood a hundred times.

Calligraphy inspired by the text

Writing

Sun

Pen

Joy

Happiness

Moon

Door

Moon

Friend

The door to love

Venus

 Hope

 Passage

 Hand

 Birds

 Nightingale

 Earth

 Garden

 Path

 Pencil box

Breath

 To charm

 Light

 Mountain

 Words

 Journey

 The secret

 The garden of love

 House

 Charmer

Charm

 The cup

 Birds

 Visible

 Invisible

 The happiness of love

 Joy

 Carnal

 Charming